SCOTTISH STEAM MISCELLANY

MISCELLANY

R. D. STEPHEN

D. BRADFORD BARTON LIMITED

Frontispiece: Dignity at Perth — two North British generations at the old NB shed — rebuilt Holmes No.9214 and Reid Atlantic No.9876 *Waverley*. [*W. D. M. Stephen*]

introduction

Like its predecessor *Scottish Steam in the 1920s,* this volume depicts the railways north of the Border through the decade from the end of the Great War into the years following the Grouping of 1923. This was a time of great change, not least after the formation of the LNER and LMS companies. The layout of the volume has been arranged in sections which either provide interesting comparisons of contemporary locomotive practice of each of the former companies or are related to some of the locations where I took the majority of my photographs. These, dating from 1920, have been chosen to illustrate the era as widely and comprehensively as possible and comprise:

Victoriana The first selection consists of five nineteenth century veterans representing each of the Scottish railways, all in rebuilt form but retaining many of their original fascinating characteristics — some to a greater degree than others. Each of them had useful service to its credit with the post-Grouping companies. Immediately after the War there were numerous obsolete engines standing in sidings at sheds and elsewhere awaiting breaking up — a notable example being a priceless Highland collection at Culloden Moor station.

Top Link The twenty-two Reid Atlantics were the undisputed express engines on the North British Railway. The same could be said of the Cumming 'Clan' on the Highland and likewise of the eight efficient Heywood 4-4-0s on the Great North of Scotland. The ultimate on the Glasgow & South Western was the Whitelegg Baltic tank intended for use on the short-distance routes between Glasgow and the Clyde Coast. Although employed on express turns between Kilmarnock and St. Enoch, the main line traffic to Carlisle was still in the hands of Manson 4-6-0s, frequently assisted. On the Caledonian, the choice lay between three 4-6-0 classes; most recently built and far ahead in power, but not performance, was Pickersgill's three-cylinder 956 class which had followed his 60 class with two cylinders. Older by far were McIntosh's Cardean class and the generally similiar but slightly older Nos. 49 and 50, a total of 16 locomotives. The McIntosh's engines were undoubtedly the most successful but, in practice, many of the heaviest main line express trains were handled by the superheated McIntosh and Pickersgill 4-4-0s, frequently working in pairs. Centres such as Aberdeen, Perth and Carlisle were excellent places for viewing these premier engines together, all so different especially in their pre-Grouping liveries.

West Fife My first railway photographs were taken at my home town of Inverkeithing, the well-known North British junction in West Fife where the main lines to Aberdeen and Perth diverged. With the exception of the Aberdeen and Perth expresses and a few Dundee semi-fasts, all passenger trains stopped at Inverkeithing where, fortunately, the station was very suitable for photography. Refuge sidings for goods trains and a large marshalling yard provided plenty of engine types and finally, there was the little family of banking engines — all obsolete classes. One disadvantage in final NB days was that stationary Atlantics, 'Scotts' and 'Glens' were few and far between, a situation which changed dramatically when the G.C. type 'Directors' came along in 1924-25. Consequently most of the stopping trains were headed by rebuilt Holmes 4-4-0s which did become a little monotonous. Included in this collection is a view of superheated 'Scott' No. 418 *Dumbiedykes*. Photographs of this class in its original condition are very rare simply because most of the class were built during the War when photography was restricted. By 1920 their appearance was being completely altered by the removal of the smokebox wingplates which on these and the 'Glens' were extremely prominent.

Near at hand was Dunfermline Upper shed which accommodated about sixty engines, mostly goods classes including three G.C. R O D type 2-8-0s for the heavy coal traffic to Aberdeen, as well as a large number of Gresley's small-wheeled J38 0-6-0s which had replaced older NB engines on the short-haul work around the West Fife coalfields. In addition there were a number of Holmes passenger engines for local passenger trains as well as tank engines for shunting and the branch line to Alloa via Kincardine on the shores of the Forth. All in all, Dunfermline Upper was an extremely interesting shed in the 1920s and many of my earliest photographic days were spent there.

Perth On a Saturday afternoon, especially in the height of the holiday season, Perth station was a very busy place. Between three and four o'clock in the afternoon there was continual movement with up and down Caledonian, Highland and North British trains all co-inciding. Most interesting was the marshalling of the Highland portions to and from Edinburgh and Glasgow for which the HR had a most attractive little 4-4-0T which — between these periodical rush hours — simply stood in a siding at the north end of the station waiting to be photographed. My first move was always to the Highland shed to photograph the engine rostered for the 3.50 p.m. to Inverness, as well as anything of interest which had come in from the north. The shed was small but housed plenty of power; on a Sunday visit to Perth in 1930 we found three 'Clans,' two 'Rivers', five 'Castles' and seven Horwich 'Crabs' as well as some smaller Highland types there. That they were all heading north gave them a purposeful look which was quite striking. A few years later the scene had changed. The 'Clans' had been transferred to the Callander and Oban line and the Stanier Class Fives had arrived, whilst 'Rivers' could be seen on Blair Atholl 'slows'.

The premier shed at Perth was the Caledonian — an important changing point. The layout was extensive and an added advantage was the turntable, very suitably placed for photography. All the leading CR types could be seen, very numerous being the superheated Dunalastairs and Pickersgill 4-4-0s which coped with most of the express traffic — singly or in pairs. Pickersgill's three-cylindered 4-6-0 No. 959 started its life there; also associated with Perth for a long time was Cardean No. 905. It is well known that the Caledonian single No. 123 (then 14010) was also stationed there in the early 1930s, running on local services to Dundee.

Chiefly owing to lack of time, the North British shed was seldom visited. Housed there in the 1920s were two 'Shire' D49 4-4-0s, one appropriately being No. 250 *Perthshire* which — supported by two 'Scotts' — took care of the main line to Edinburgh, while for the North of Fife and Devon Valley lines there were a number of Holmes rebuilt 4-4-0s. Unfortunately, however, Perth General station was not very suitable for photography and so all the interesting things that happened there remained unrecorded.

Drummond Tanks Scotland was the birthplace of the Drummond tank engine and a brief selection of six photographs recalls memories of an engine family which could be found on four of the Scottish railways, the exception being the Great North of Scotland. Whether designed by Dugald Drummond or his brother Peter, their styling varied very little. Particularly attractive were the two small NB and CR engines with their solid bogie wheels.

Edinburgh & Glasgow In 1924 schooldays changed to an office life in Leith and, with only Saturday afternoons and two weeks holiday a year available, somewhere better for photography than Inverkeithing had to be found. Haymarket shed was unsuitable owing to the end-on position of the sun in the afternoons and the answer to the problem proved to be Craigentinny carriage sidings adjacent to the East Coast main line a short distance south of Waverley. In addition to the normal movements of empty stock to and from Waverley, there were numerous Saturday special trains, very popular in those days. To add to the interest, most of the empty stock was handled by main line engines, some of which — including Atlantics and 'Directors' — were serviced in special sidings. A further Saturday afternoon bonus was a steady procession of goods engines and shunting tanks from the various marshalling yards finding their way to St. Margarets shed for the weekend.

The variety of subjects was excellent and, provided there was a steady west wind keeping smoke and steam out of the way, an afternoon at Craigentinny was most enjoyable.

Frequently visited was Eastfield shed, quickly reached from Edinburgh by the 1 p.m. from Waverley which, very conveniently, commenced its journey at Leith Central station. For good measure it was one of those trains which, to facilitate a return working, changed engines at Cowlairs station, the train continuing to Queen Street behind one of the ubiquitous 0-6-2T banking engines. By walking along the line from Cowlairs station one could be at Eastfield in just over the hour from Edinburgh. By far the largest shed in the Southern Scottish area of the LNER, it had much to offer, and with engines from outside depots waiting to go to Cowlairs for repairs in addition to the normal daily programme of the shed, the choice was almost unlimited. Particularly attractive were engines fresh from the paint shop awaiting return to their home sheds — always in good supply at the weekend. The shed staff was most co-operative and I can remember an occasion when, not only was a line of six newly painted engines moved from inside the shed, but each was posed separately for photographing. Mention should also be made of the 'Glens' allocated to the West Highland line, seldom seen east of Glasgow, also the Gresley K2 2-6-0s bearing Loch names. An afternoon at Eastfield invariably ended in a footplate run down to Queen Street.

G & SWR Regrettably, my contact with the Glasgow & South Western was somewhat limited, largely because of its geographical position plus my lack of time, although in fact Corkerhill shed would have been just as accessible as Eastfield. Admittedly, permission to visit an LMS shed was not so readily available as on the LNER. However a few photographs have been selected from a G & SWR shed visit I made in 1927 to Hurlford. This, near Kilmarnock, was one of the most important sheds on the South Western but unfortunately on the occasion of this visit in 1927 neither a Manson 4-6-0 nor a Whitelegg Baltic was to be seen.

Highland Holidays The annual summer holiday was invariably in the Highlands and many profitable days were spent with the camera at Blair Atholl, Aviemore, Dingwall and, not least, Inverness. The main quest was for the older Highland classes which in the 1920s were fast disappearing. In 1921 Blair Atholl housed four of Peter Drummond's large 0-6-4Ts for banking up to Dalnaspidal and two of Jones' 'Straths', Nos. 97 and 99 *Glenmore* and *Glentromie*, used on the local trains to Perth. Also there was No. 76A *Bruce*, one of the Clyde Bogies built in 1886. Goods trains were always banked but the usual custom with passenger trains was to put the assisting engine at the front and it was chiefly for this duty that *Bruce* was stationed there. The following year both 'Straths' were replaced by a 'Loch' and a small 'Ben', although *Bruce* was to remain for another season.

In addition to its importance as a junction, Aviemore was the home of quite a large number of engines used for assisting trains to Dalwhinnie in the south as well as, to a lesser degree, Slochd summit on the direct line to Inverness and to Dava on the Forres route. In August 1924 five 'Lochs' and three small 'Bens' were stationed there for these duties. A sign of the times was *Strathspey* and two of the earlier 'Duke' class 4-4-0s, *Atholl* and *Dochfour*, lying idle in a siding.

Dingwall's chief attraction were the Skye bogies which, until 1927 at least, were still hard at work on the Kyle of Lochalsh line, although it was at Inverness that most of the older engines were to be seen latterly. Notable among these were the little Stroudley six-coupled tanks and two of the outside-cylindered 4-4-0Ts shunting in the station. On a visit to Inverness in 1930 only two veterans remained — a Skye Bogie, No. 14284, and Stroudley tank No. 16119, formerly *Lochgorm*.

The other Scottish railway associated with the Highlands was the Great North of Scotland of which I saw a great deal in its last days, during several annual visits to Kittybrewster. One holiday was spent at Ballater on the Deeside line where I was fortunate in obtaining photographs of various Royal Train engines in all their splendour.

As regards cameras, my first photographs were taken with a very simple camera purchased in 1919 at a cost of £3.12.6 — a folding Kodak with picture size of 2½″ × 4¼″. This was fitted with one of the first examples of the double lens called a Rapid Rectilinear — commonly referred to as an RR. It gave excellent results except at the margins, its widest aperture being equivalent to f8. By stopping down and not going too close to the subject, the marginal defects of the lens could be avoided but with the very slow films available over fifty years ago there had to be a golden rule that bright sunshine was absolutely essential. The negatives have kept remarkably well, especially as many of the earlier ones were commercially developed locally: later we did our own developing. In 1925 a Goerz Tenax hand camera with anastigmatic lens was acquired and finally a quarter-plate Popular Pressman Reflex with Ross Xpres lens which, with panchromatic plates, gave beautiful negatives. With this it was also possible to photograph moving trains.

My railway photography in Britain ceased in 1930, as in that year I accepted a post in Singapore and was to remain in the East for some twenty years. With the improved film material and more generous spare time of later years, my collection would otherwise have been considerably greater.

Bolton-le-Sands
Carnforth

R. D. Stephen

Still in passenger service and standing at Inverkeithing in July 1926, only a few months before withdrawal, No. 10249 was one of Thomas Wheatley's 2-4-0s as rebuilt by W. P. Reid in 1915 — their second rebuilding. Fitted with standard boilers, the addition of the side-window cab brought the appearance of these smart little engines completely into line with the various NB 4-4-0 classes, although the large leading wheels and small tenders (weighing about 26 tons) were vivid reminders of their early history — a class of eight engines dating back to 1873, their first reconstruction being by Matthew Holmes in 1890/91. The decision to give six of these very small engines yet another lease of life, prompted largely by war-time restrictions on supplies of new material, paid dividends as their total wheelbase (32ft. 4½in.) was admirable on minor branch lines with short turntables. Stationed latterly at Burntisland, No.10249's final workings were on passenger trains between Thornton and Inverkeithing, in addition to night banking duties there. All six engines entered LNER ownership — class E7 — the last to go being No.10247 in 1927.

In 1888/91 Dugald Drummond produced a 5ft. 9in. coupled wheel version of his most successful express engine for the steeply-graded Greenock line but No.1114, photographed at Stirling in August 1926, was then employed on banking duties. Still in Caledonian blue, the engine was very little altered from the original, the main difference being the absence of smokebox wingplates.

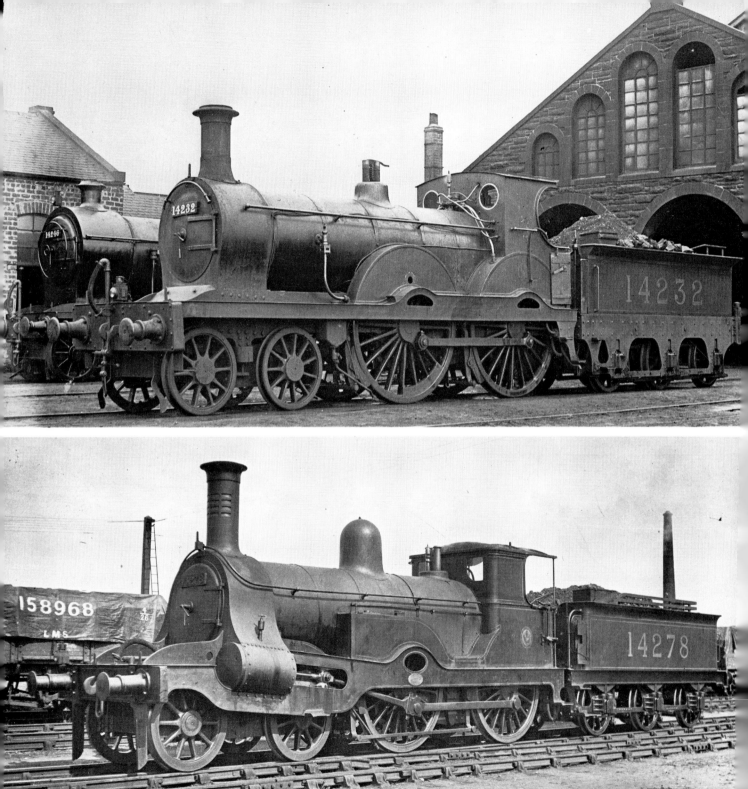

The nineteenth century representative of the Great North of Scotland Railway was the well known Cowan 4-4-0 No. 45A of 1866, one of three of the class which came into the LNER in 1523. Its last years were spent shunting ash wagons at Kittybrewster shed, where it was photographed in September 1923, the small four-wheel tender (holding 2 tons of coal and 1050 gallons of water) being a reminder that she was always available as spare for the Alford branch, which had a short turntable. In 1925 No. 45A, specially repainted in Great North green, appeared at the Darlington Centenary Celebrations with a train of contemporary coaches but very unfortunately was withdrawn soon after — then the last engine on a Scottish railway to have a brass dome.

Another veteran of 1873 was Glasgow & South Western 4-4-0 No. 14232, one of James Stirling's celebrated 4-4-0s, 22 of which were built at Kilmarnock in 1873-7. Most successful and a great advance on their 0-4-2 predecessors, for several years they handled from Carlisle all the heavy Midland trains coming through from St. Pancras until they were replaced by more advanced Smellie designs. No 14232, photographed at Hurlford in the summer of 1927, was one of sixteen of the class rebuilt by Manson in 1899-1901 and, although considerably altered in the process, the compact engine wheelbase, safety valves on boiler barrel and outside-framed tender remained as great attractions for the locomotive photographer. They were doing passenger work well into LMS days and the last of the class is reported as withdrawn in 1930.

No. 14278, standing at Forres in August 1926, was one of David Jones' express engines for the Highland Railway with 6'3" coupled wheels and 18" × 24" cylinders, a design originating in 1874 and finally totalling 25 engines. One of a series of eight engines built in 1886 by the Clyde Locomotive Co. and consequently known as the 'Clyde Bogies', No. 14278 as HR No. 82 latterly carried the name *Durn* (the residence of the then Deputy Chairman of the Company) but this was transferred to Christopher Cumming's new 4-4-0 No. 74 in 1917. In common with all the Jones engines, the engine was fitted with louvred chimney, in this case capped in later years with a Drummond top. No. 14278 was broken up in 1930, outliving others of the class by five years. Her last passenger workings were on the branch line from Orbliston Junction to Fochabers.

11

TOP LINK

North British Atlantic No. 877 *Liddesdale* looking extremely handsome at Inverkeithing in 1920; although this photograph has the margin defects of the RR lens, referred to in the Introduction, it is the only one showing one of the original Atlantics of 1906 before their rebuilding with superheaters. As originally constructed, the running plate narrowed aft of the cylinders, as on the Great Central Atlantics, but when superheated from 1915 onwards, this was increased to full width, providing a wider cab with improved lookout ahead. Among other differences from the final Atlantic were the small dome, rounded cylinder casing and absence of mechanical lubricator. Stationary Atlantics were most uncommon at Inverkeithing but *Liddesdale* was on a filling-in turn which involved a morning local from Edinburgh to Dunfermline Lower, returning light engine direct to Waverley, where it was rostered for the 10.05 a.m. Aberdeen express. On occasions the engine had to refuge at Inverkeithing for a short time and this was one of them.

Much has been written over the years about McIntosh's famous 'Cardean' class for the Caledonian Railway, five o which were built at St. Rollox in 1906. Enhanced by their vast 57-ton bogie tenders, they were magnificent looking engines, especially in Caledonian livery. In 1915 No. 907, the last of the class, was broken up as a result o heavy damage sustained at the Quintinshill disaster. This reduced the number to four engines, two of which ra between Glasgow and Carlisle, and the others on the Aberdeen road. No. 905, being turned at Perth in 1921 fo another trip to Aberdeen, differed from others of the class in having Ross Pop safety valves, also a large diamete air-cooled Westinghouse pump.

No. 54 *Southesk,* coaling at Kittybrewster in 1921, illustrates the final GNSR express engine design, eight of which appeared in 1920-21. The first six came from the North British Locomotive Co, and my first view of No. 54 — then without a name — was at Inverkeithing, next to the brakevan of a goods train *en route* to Aberdeen. Two further engines were built at Inverurie and all eight were eventually named. No. 54 took its name from the Earl of Southesk, a director of the company. Small but efficient, these engines remained the principal ones for express work on Great North territory until the early 1930s, when a number of ex-Great Eastern B12 4-6-0s came north to deal with trains which were then composed of heavy Gresley buckeye-coupling rolling stock.

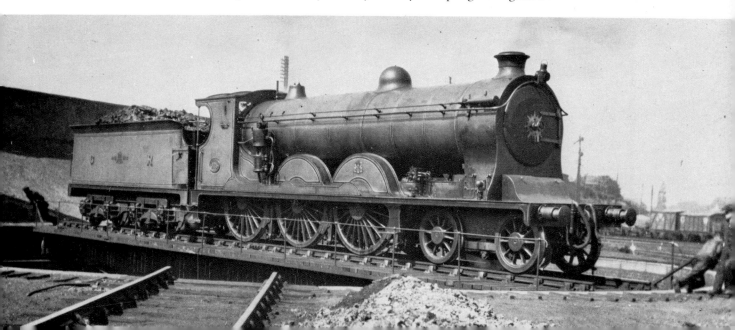

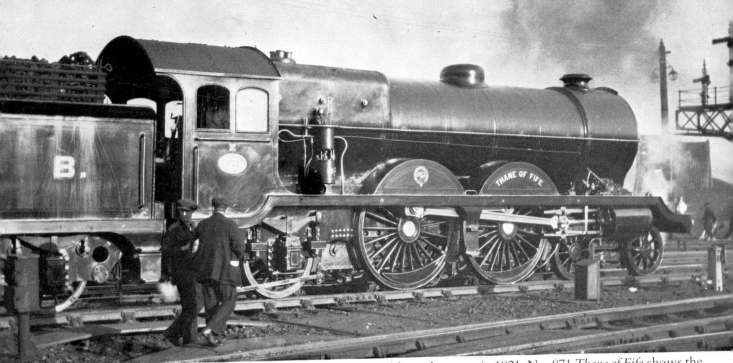

Facing into the evening sun at Aberdeen Joint station on a southbound express in 1921, No. 871 *Thane of Fife* shows the Reid Atlantic in its final NB state after rebuilding with superheater. The wider running plate and cab with side windows nearer the roof edge, also the larger dome, are obvious when compared with *Liddesdale* on page 12. The massive trailing wheels carried a weight of 19 tons 1 cwt. The Atlantics were noted for their splendid names which cleverly represented the entire North British territory, commencing with No. 868 *Aberdonian* and working south systematically to Carlisle, No. 871 deriving its name from a Fife nobleman of earlier times and prominent in Shakespeare's 'Macbeth'. It was very pleasing that many of their names were perpetuated in the Peppercorn A1 Pacifics, *Thane of Fife*, for instance, going to one of Gresley's celebrated 2-8-2 'Cock o' the North' class.

Clan Cameron at Perth, on the turntable at the North shed, looking very fresh in the unlined Highland green livery relieved by what always seemed a very bright red bufferbeam, with the No. 57 in bold gilt lettering. Eight engines of the 'Clan' class were built by Hawthorn, Leslie, *Clan Cameron* being the last to appear in 1921, the date of this photograph. Barely two tons heavier than the final 'Castle' — Smith's three engines built with 6' driving wheels — they were allowed an additional 30 tons on the Druimochdar and Slochd banks unassisted and considerably more on the less onerous sections. This photograph was taken with my earliest camera, well back from the subject, so that marginal lack of definition has been avoided. The signal box in the background, since removed, shows true 'Caledonian' architecture.

No. 540, the first of Whitelegg's splendid Baltics of 1922 for the Glasgow & South Western Railway, turning on the triangle at St. Enoch. The handsome profile, beautiful finish and shapely lettering are very evident. This photograph, taken shortly after the engines were built, recalls the drivers' extreme pride in them and their unwillingness to accept any criticism about them, at any rate from a layman. Time showed that the Baltics had many failings but undoubtedly these would have been taken in hand had the Grouping not come along so soon after their introduction.

WEST FIFE

The most spectacular North British express was undoubtedly the 7.35 a.m. Edinburgh-Aberdeen which, with through coaches from Kings Cross and St. Pancras, invariably loaded to fourteen vehicles. Added on Sundays was the through service from Penzance to Aberdeen, for which the NB built special 1st/3rd/van composites, one of which is seen at the head of the train. No.874 *Dunedin* and No.339 *Ivanhoe,* an unrebuilt 'Scott', made a brief stop at Inverkeithing in April 1922 to allow the Earl of Elgin, a director of the NB, to alight. Less than a year later *Dunedin,* repainted in NB bronze green, but with L&NER and number on tender in NB style transfers, was one of eight pre-Grouping engines painted in their old liveries for inspection by the Board at York on 31 January 1923 with a view to deciding upon one colour scheme for the future.

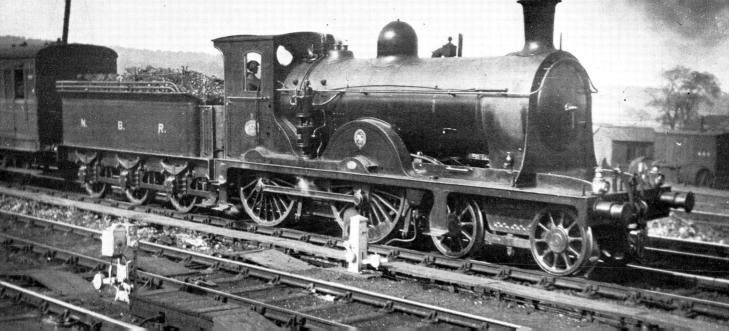

Matthew Holmes' chief goods engine design for the NB was a large class of 0-6-0s totalling 168 engines, built between 1888-1900. All were rebuilt by W. P. Reid, or his successor Walter Chalmers, the only significant changes being slightly larger boilers and the usual side-window cab. The view of No. 711, standing beside Inverkeithing Central Signal Box with its brake van, is a real North British period piece. Classed J36 by the LNER, they had a long life, No. 711 lasting until January 1966. There still remains *Maude*, NB No. 673, one of 25 of the class which saw service in France in the 1914-18 War, and now in the care of the Scottish Railway Preservation Society.

A Stirling-Edinburgh train at Inverkeithing in 1921 hauled by 4-4-0 No. 592, one of Matthew Holmes' twelve express engines with 7' driving wheels built between 1886-88. In their early days they were very much in the limelight. No. 592 was exhibited at the Edinburgh International Exhibition in 1886, part of the journey to the Exhibition grounds being along the streets under her own steam, using movable sections of temporary track. Another celebrity was No. 602, the Royal Train engine at the opening of the Forth Bridge on 4 June 1890. All were rebuilt by Reid in 1911 with new boilers with most gracefully tapered chimneys, while the Holmes Stirling-type open cab was replaced by the standard side-window style. In keeping with later policy, smokebox wingplates were removed. Final years were spent on local services and as pilots at Haymarket shed. The departure of the 6.35 p.m. Aberdeen express from the centre of the roofed-over Waverley station behind an Atlantic and 'seven-footer' was a sight and sound never to be forgotten. No. 592 was withdrawn in 1932 — as LNER Class D25 No. 9592.

One of the few photographs secured before the large tender numerals became universal on the NB was this one of No. 579, a Holmes 4-4-0 as rebuilt by Reid in 1911. One of Holmes' first series of 4-4-0s, six engines built in 1884, they were smaller than the two classes that followed but all were formed into one class when rebuilt by Reid with his standard boilers. No. 579 is seen waiting to leave Inverkeithing for Edinburgh with a train from Rosyth Dockyard, in 1920.

Photographed at Inverkeithing North Sidings, after engine and tender had found themselves going in different directions, is rebuilt Holmes 4-4-0 No. 262. Turned out in November 1894, No. 262 made history nine months later in the Railway Races, when on 22 August 1895 it achieved the fastest timing from Dundee to Aberdeen – 71.3 miles in 77 minutes, admittedly with a very light train. One of the 48 engines classed D31 by the LNER, it was broken up in 1937.

Holmes' final design was his 317 class 4-4-0s, twelve of which were built about the time of his death in 1903. No. 321 is shown on an Edinburgh-Dundee train at Inverkeithing in April 1922, seven months before withdrawal. They were a great advance on his earlier 4-4-0s. With longer boilers, resulting in an extended wheelbase and a boiler pressure of 200lbs. per sq. in., they were the most powerful express engines to date on the NB. By 1922, having been superseded by Reid's larger designs, it was decided not to fit them with new boilers, and so ended the 'Holmes-rebuilt-by-Reid' era. Nine of these engines became Class D26 in the LNER, the last to be withdrawn being No. 9325 in July 1926. They were the first locomotives to have the single side-window cab, a design feature which, apart from the Atlantics, was to become universal on the NB right to the end.

Another mishap at Inverkeithing, with the main line completely blocked at the Central Junction due to a goods train backing on the down main line, splitting cross-over points. The 36-ton St. Margarets crane has just arrived to assist the Thornton 15-ton one which, owing to the elevation of the curve, had re-railed three of the wagons only with great difficulty. The striking junction signal, with its typically positioned 'calling-on arms', remained until the 1960s, when an improved road for approaches to the new Forth Road Bridge enabled the layout to be improved for faster running.

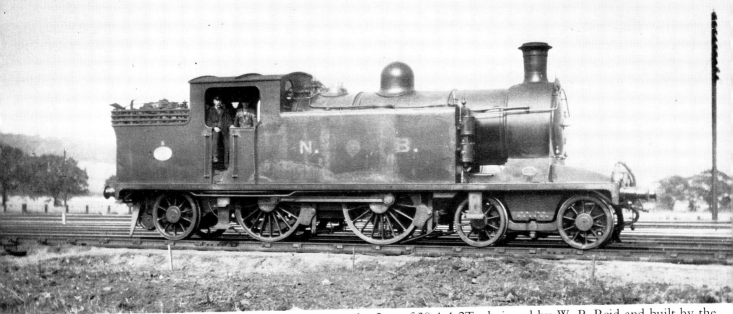

The final NB engine to carry the number one was the first of 30 4-4-2Ts designed by W. P. Reid and built by the Yorkshire Engine Co in 1911-13. Although these locomotives had the same tracive effort as his 0-4-4T of 1909, and indeed shared the same boiler, their increased water and coal capacity was a great step forward. No. 1, long overdue for a repaint, was photographed at Inverkeithing in 1920. The Westinghouse pump sited on the tank front of the first eleven engines was later shifted to the side of the smokebox, bringing them into line with those built subsequently, no doubt to facilitate oiling between the frames. The last two survivors were employed on the Craigendoran-Arrochar push-and-pull services until replaced in 1960 by a diesel rail-bus.

Also at the same shed is Holmes 0-6-0T No. 808, one of a class of 40 engines built by outside contractors in 1900-01. All were rebuilt in 1924-25, the main external difference being the shifting of the safety valves from dome to firebox. Classed J83 by the LNER, they had a long and useful life and were to be seen all over former NB territory. Perhaps their best known location was Waverley station, where they carried out shunting operations for some 30 years until replaced by diesels. Many continued in service until 1962.

Recently repainted is Holmes 0-4-4T No. 94, built in 1889 and — despite a rebuild in 1912 — little altered from the original. It was one of twelve engines produced between 1886-89, the last passenger tanks to be introduced on the NB for 20 years. No. 94 was photographed at Dunfermline Upper shed in September 1922; on the coaling stage line is a rebuilt Holmes 0-6-0, later Class J36.

Standing in the same siding four years later, and just back from Cowlairs equipped with Westinghouse brake, is ex-GN 4-4-0 No.3052, one of Ivatt's final superheated 4-4-0s, built in 1911; the entire class of 15 engines was transferred to the Southern Scottish Area in 1925 to replace old NB types. Not powerful enough to take their place with the Reid passenger classes, they were employed on minor local services for which they had to be Westinghouse fitted for use on older rolling stock. Working from Haymarket shed, they proved very able pilots on the Aberdeen line.

hotographed at Dunfermline Upper shed in 1923, awaiting despatch to Cowlairs for overhaul, rebuilt Wheatley 2-4-0 No.1249 is still in NB livery. Built in 1873 as No.428, and bearing the name *Ratho* in Drummond days, this engine became No.1249 on the NB duplicate list in 1915. For a short time in 1924, under a Cowlairs re-numbering scheme later discarded, the number 9990 was carried, finally to be altered to 10249 and as such the engine is referred to at the beginning of this volume.

Larger passenger engines were seldom seen at Dunfermline Upper shed in the early 1920s, except on special workings. No. 100 *Glen Dochart*, a visitor in 1923, shows a 'Glen' exactly as built, before their appearance was so radically altered by the removal of the prominent smokebox wingplates. The small fixture on top of the smokebox was for a pyrometer, for measuring the temperature of steam in the header which was fitted on all new superheated engines built for the NBR but discarded after the Grouping.

Holmes 4-4-0 No.729, the first of its class built in 1898, photographed on an Edinburgh-Stirling train at Inverkeithing, shortly after rebuilding in 1921. Despite its age, this negative has produced a satisfactory enlargement, a fitting tribute to a beautifully turned-out engine, which is enhanced by the star on the smokebox door and the polished edge on the smokebox itself.

26

This section devoted to West Fife concludes as it began, with the 7.35 a.m. Edinburgh-Aberdeen express, this time photographed in 1925, with motive power little dreamed of three years earlier. GC 'Director' No.6401 *James Fitzjames* and ex-GN 4-4-0 No.3051 had certainly built up good reserves of steam on the run down from the Forth Bridge. Behind the precariously located six-wheel saloon is the through portion from Kings Cross, followed by the NB steel dining car, four coaches from St. Pancras and, finally, some NB vehicles from Edinburgh. The whole resulted in a most varied and heavy train.

PERTH

Pickersgill's first design for the Caledonian was an express passenger 4-4-0, first built in 1916 and very similar in main dimensions to superheated Dunalastair IV class but differing quite considerably in constructional details. Outwardly the main visual differences were the absence of smokebox wingplates, the straight upper edge to the coupling rod splashers and a very stylish single-casting chimney. Although McIntosh's final engines, the heavy mixed traffic 179 4-6-0 class, had been provided with side-window cabs, Pickersgill reverted to the traditional CR open type, rather strangely as it was he who had introduced the GNSR to the comforts of a windowed cab as long ago as 1899. No.14489 was photographed at Perth in 1925 at a time when these engines were in their prime. A year earlier, one of the class had taken part in dynamometer tests with comparable LMS types between Leeds and Carlisle.

Also on the turntable at Perth is 4-4-0 No.138, one of the final batch of '140' or 'Dunalastair IV' class built in 1910 and numbered 136-138. This was the last new McIntosh 4-4-0 produced to use saturated steam, the following engine (No.139) being the first superheated engine in Scotland. The final design of bogie tender weighing 56 tons, carrying six tons of coal and 4,600 gallons of water, with independent axle springing, appeared for the first time on these four engines.

No. 383, a very sturdy Drummond design of 0-6-0 saddle tank, two of which were stationed at Perth until about 1922; they were then replaced by the McIntosh standard shunting tanks, one of which is visible in this photograph. One drawback of the design was that the cab bunker left little room on the footplate for the driver and fireman.

To complete the true Caledonian scene at Perth is a McIntosh standard goods 0-6-0, No.878, the last of a class of 79 engines built 1899-1900. Originally termed 'mixed traffic' engines, some were fitted with Westinghouse brakes and painted blue for work on the Clyde Coast trains. In 1922, No.878 was in the goods livery, black with red and white lining. Some of these engines were among the last former CR types to run on British Railways.

Another Drummond engine, 0-4-0 saddle tank *Pug,* No.1265, was used on the Harbour branch on the River Tay. The first of these useful little engines was built in 1885, further additions being made by McIntosh as late as 1908. Note the old-fashioned cast-iron wheels with T-section spokes. With negligible room on the footplate for coal, a small wooden truck serving as a tender was generally attached, access to this being via a small opening in the panel at the rear of the footplate.

A Perth-Edinburgh train at Inverkeithing in 1922, hauled by superheated 'Scott' 4-4-0 No.418 *Dumbiedykes*. Named after a character in Scott's 'Heart of Midlothian', *Dumbiedykes* and No.270 *Glen Garry* were the premier express engines at the small NB shed at Perth for many years, being replaced by two Scottish 'Directors' in 1925. The absence of paint on the smokebox wingplates was due to the driver having started to remove this in an attempt to simulate an engine from which the wingplates had been removed, a practice just started on the North British. Two of the reverse curves at Inverkeithing station, which necessitated a speed restriction of 20 mph, show clearly in this photograph.

No. 14655 was one of Pickersgill's 60 class 4-6-0s, built in 1916–17, which in the 1920s were still doing first-class work on the Aberdeen road. Differing considerably from the McIntosh 4-6-0s, they had outside cylinders, the first Caledonian main line engines so fitted since the little Oban bogies of 1882. With 20″ × 26″ cylinders and 6′1″ driving wheels, they were powerful and fine-looking engines although not outstandingly successful in performance. Nevertheless, a further twenty of them, slightly modified, were built by the LMS in 1925-26.

Photographs of the 'Rivers' and 'Clans' built by Hawthorn, Leslie in 1915 and 1919-21 respectively, make an interesting comparison. As is well known, the 'Rivers', failing to receive clearance from the HR Engineers Dept were sold to the Caledonian, only to return to their native heath when the LMS took over. Leading dimensions of both classes were more or less identical, the main difference being that the 'Clan' had a boiler 5″ less in diameter contributing to a saving in weight of about 10 tons and resulting in what might be termed a scaled down version of the 'River'. Their appearances differed considerably, the latter favouring a high running plate after the Urie fashion of the LSWR whilst the motion of the 'Clan' was partly concealed by a long casing resembling NER practice, No 14759, and 14762 Clan Campbell, photographed at Perth in 1928, recall the considerable variety of 4-6-0s to be seen there before the days of the Stanier Black Fives.

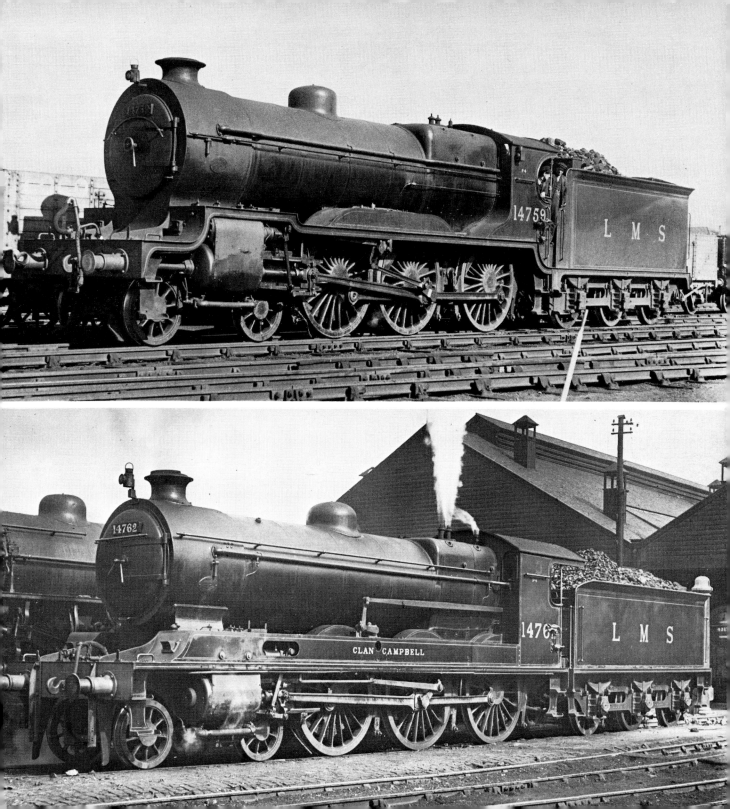

The Derby compound 4-4-0 was making its presence felt increasingly at Perth in the late 1920s, exhaustive tests by the LMS having established that on trains loading up to 350 tons, it was more efficient than the various Caledonian 4-6-0 classes. The 4-4-0s had a powerful and very symmetrical appearance, very evident in this broadside profile of No.1184. This has the pure Derby chimney reduced in height, together with the dome, for service in Scotland. These were the only striking differences in outline from No.1000, restored to its 1914 state and now at York Museum. In later years, Stanier-pattern chimneys were fitted to these engines.

No.14388 *Loch Luichart* was one of David Jones 'Loch' class built in 1896, some of which, together with the small Bens, were in charge of the local services between Perth and Blair Atholl. Unlike many of the class, which were rebuilt by the LMS with the higher-pitched CR 'N' type boiler, this engine had retained one of the original pattern, thus looking very much as built except for the Drummond chimney and removal of wingplates. This view at Aviemore in June 1930 — with my brother W. D. M. Stephen on the footplate — has been selected as a suitable companion to face the similarly placed Compound which with the Lochs were the only outside cylindered 4-4-0s at the time in LMS Scottish service apart from a handful of earlier ex-Highland engines and No.14509 *Lord Glenarthur,* the unique Whitelegg rebuild of a Manson 4-cylinder compound 4-4-0.

No. 14522 *Snaigow,* the first of Cumming's two 4-4-0s built in 1917, waiting at the ticket platform at the North end of Perth General *en route* to take over a semi-fast for Aviemore in the summer of 1929. This was one of those occasions when a unique subject, bright sunshine and a signal at danger all came together. These two engines were built specially for the heavy war-time naval traffic between Inverness and Thurso and with a load classification of their own — 'P' — in the Northern Division, were permitted to take 25 tons more than their immediate predecessors, the 'Lochs'. Displaced by 'Castles' and gradually moving down the scale, they were finally stationed at Aviemore, working as pilots as well as on trips to Inverness and Perth. *Snaigow,* the last to be broken up in 1936, bore the name of the estate of W. H. Cox, Chairman of the Highland Railway from 1917 until its dissolution in 1923.

Seen at Perth in 1929 is the famous Caledonian 7′ single in LMS red livery. Better known as CR No. 123, and a design by Neilson & Co. based on the contemporary Drummond 4-4-0 of the 66 Class, it was built in 1886 and appeared the same year at the Edinburgh Exhibition. Thereafter it was purchased by the Caledonian Railway and put into service between Glasgow and Carlisle, where it distinguished itself in the first Railway Races of 1888. On one occasion, with a train of 80 tons, it covered the 100 miles between Carlisle and Edinburgh in exactly 102.33 minutes. For many years No. 123 was seldom seen on the line, apart from infrequent trips with the Directors' Saloon but in the late 1920s it was restored to revenue-earning service on the level run along the River Tay from Perth to Dundee. Preserved in blue livery at Glasgow Transport Museum and with a slightly more modern boiler, the Caley single looks very much as she did in her most glorious days.

McIntosh's final design for the Caledonian, a mixed traffic 4-6-0 with 5'9" coupled driving wheels and 19½" × 26" cylinders, was rather overshadowed as regards publicity by the Pickersgill engines which followed. Eleven of the former were built at St. Rollox in 1913-14 and No. 17913 at Perth shows them to be fine, powerful-looking engines enhanced by an ample cab with two side windows, a feature which was not repeated by Pickersgill. The '179' Class, as they were designated by the CR, was chiefly employed on heavy goods traffic between Carlisle and the Central Area.

An attraction for enthusiasts at Perth was the little 4-4-0T which attended to the shunting on the Highland side of the station for many years. No. 15012, formerly well known as HR No. 50B, was one of three built by David Jones between 1878-9 as 2-4-0Ts, but fitted with bogies two years later, the front end weight on a single axle proving excessive. Originally intended for shunting, they were put on to branch line working in their early days, No. 50B, carrying the name *Aberfeldy*, on which branch it saw service, latterly as spare engine. The remaining two engines, Nos. 15010 and 15011, also ended their service on passenger shunting — at Inverness — the class becoming extinct in 1932.

The Caledonian shunting at Perth was also undertaken by a 4-4-0T, No. 15026. This was one of twelve condensing tanks designed by John Lambie for the Central Underground line in Glasgow soon after he took over at St. Rollox in 1891. These had been displaced by later McIntosh 0-4-4Ts, also fitted with condensing apparatus. The cab recessed between tank and bunker appears a little odd but this did at least provide a platform for the Westinghouse pump, which was on the fireman's side.

A Perth–Blair Atholl local leaving Killiecrankie on a summer afternoon in 1927, hauled by 4-4-0 No. 14413 *Ben Alligan*, one of the twenty small Bens built by Peter Drummond between 1898 and 1906. Not reboilered as were most of the class this engine, seen in its original condition, was broken up in 1933. Behind the trees on the right is the entrance to the Pass of Killiecrankie, through which the train had just travelled, while in the far distance are the slopes of Ben Vrackie, the mountain which dominates Pitlochry.

43

DRUMMOND TANKS

Drummond's first design for the North British after his appointment in 1875 was a small 0-6-0T, 25 of which were built at Cowlairs between 1875-78. To all intents and purposes they were enlarged versions of the Brighton 'Terriers', Drummond having had some of his earlier training under Stroudley. Intended for passenger work, they were named after the localities in which they operated — which involved some changing of names from time to time. All names were subsequently removed by Holmes. With one exception, the entire class passed to the LNER but by 1926 only four remained in active service as Class J82. No.10358 — one time No. 313 *Clydebank/Musselburgh* — is seen at North Leith in June 1926, two months before withdrawal.

From 1880-84, Cowlairs built 30 of the neatest little tank engines ever to run in Britain, one of their most attractive features being solid bogie wheels. These were Drummond's last tank engine design for the NBR and, like the 0-6-0T predecessors from which they took over, originally carried names. No.1426 (formerly No.101 *Anstruther*) photographed at Dunfermline Lower in September 1923, worked on the short branch to Charlestown on the shore of the Forth. The small cast plates on the bunker side are the LNER number plate in the centre, above this the NB load classification — in this case 'R' — while at the bottom is the Cowlairs building plate. The last 4-4-0Ts in this country, they had a long life, the remaining three being broken up in 1933. For a time, some worked on the GNSR Fraserburgh-St. Combs branch, for which they were fitted with cowcatchers.

n Drummond's small passenger tank for the ⋯ ⋯ rsed, resulting in a -4-4T, slightly heavier and carrying a little mo⋯ ⋯ St. Rollox from 1884 o 1891. No. 1175, still in CR blue, was photog⋯ ⋯ n acting as spare for the Killin branch. The brackets below the bufferbear⋯ ⋯ ny sheepcatchers – required n the Leadhills & Wanlockhead Light Railway, ⋯ ⋯ on the West Coast Main line. In omparing the NB and CR designs, it is interesti⋯ ⋯ ence in the shaping of the lips of the nnels which was maintained on successive engin⋯ ⋯ es right to the end.

No. 15303 represented Peter Drummond's final design for the Highland Railway, eight of these fine 0-6-4Ts being built by the North British Locomotive Co. between 1909 and 1912. Intended also for local goods traffic, they were better known as banking engines and normally at least four were stationed at Blair Atholl for assisting up to Druimochdar. No. 15303, at Blair Atholl shed in April 1927, is in the LMS passenger red which Lochgorm applied to these engines. The last was broken up, after a strenuous life, in 1936

Dugald Drummond having left for the LSWR, the next Drummond tank engine was his brother Peter's four 0-4-4Ts built at Lochgorm Works in 1905-6. Small engines, weighing only 35 tons 15 cwt, they were admirable for the light traffic on the HR's minor branches. No. 25 *Strathpeffer*, still painted green, heads the branch train at Dingwall Junction in August 1926. Two of these engines, employed on the Dornoch branch well into British Railways days, were the last Highland Railway engines on regular active service in this country. They were replaced on the Dornoch branch by Pannier 0-6-0Ts from Swindon.

The last Drummond tank for service in Scotland was a class of 0-6-2Ts built by the North British Locomotive Co. for the G&SWR in 1915-17. Powerful engines, they were very similar to his HR 0-6-4Ts. No. 16911 was photographed at Hurlford in August 1927. As on Dugald Drummond's engines on the LSWR, the traditional, built-up chimney had given place to a very neat single casting. Before being withdrawn in 1936-47, some of these engines followed their 0-6-4T predecessors on banking duties from Blair Atholl.

Photographed at Haymarket shed in the spring of 1925, and barely seven months old, No.2569 — later to be named *Gladiateur* — was one of the first purely LNER Gresley Pacifics built in 1924-25. Twenty came from the North British Locomotive Co. and a similar number from Doncaster. No.2569 was one of the Glasgow-built engines, fifteen of which were fitted with Westinghouse brake equipment and allocated to the North Eastern Area, the remaining five with customary vacuum brake going to Haymarket for East Coast workings to Newcastle. The advent of these engines was destined to replace the Atlantics on the entire main line from London to Aberdeen.

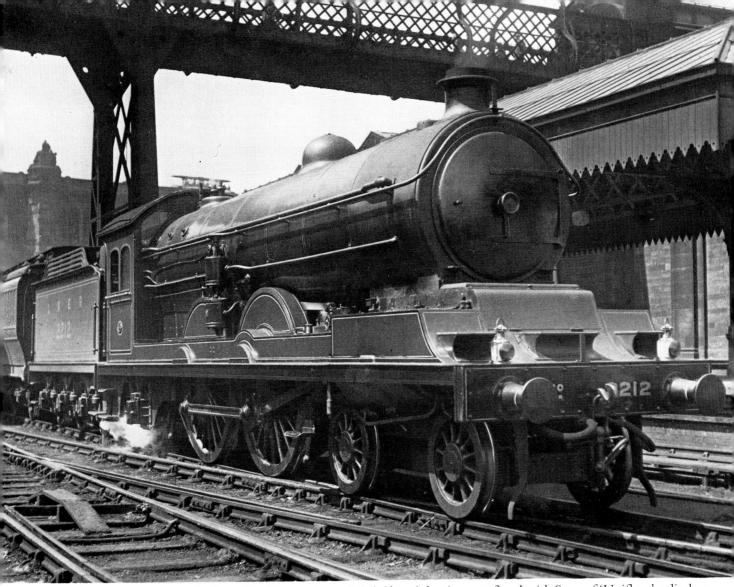

Built in 1919, No. 2212, the last of Sir Vincent Raven's 'Z' Class Atlantics, was fitted with Stumpf 'Uniflow' cylinders, his similarly equipped S.2 4-6-0 No. 825 built in 1913 having proved quite successful. This system, popular on the Continent, called for very long cylinders, entailing considerable modifications to the front end footplating which may be compared with that of the normal 'Z' on page 53. This interesting engine took its place with the other Atlantics from the North Eastern Area and, a frequent visitor to Edinburgh, is seen in 1928, coupled to a N E mail van standing beside the suburban platforms (later to be numbered 20 and 21) outside the main part of Waverley.

An early record of a Great Northern Atlantic in Edinburgh was shortly after the first War when I have recollections of a large Ivatt Atlantic passing south through Waverley in shop grey and minus dome cover — most essential for the NB loading gauge — after a commercial overhaul in Glasgow. Early in the Grouping however, large Ivatt Atlantic No. 1447 with reduced boiler mountings and cab was engaged in tests with a North Eastern three-cylinder 'Z' and an NB Atlantic, between Newcastle and Edinburgh. Later the booster-fitted Atlantic No. 4419 had a period in Scotland also undergoing tests. Unfortunately I was unable to photograph any of these occasions but this photograph of No. 4439 is included to complete this trio of East Coast Atlantics.

North Eastern Atlantic No. 705 turning on the triangle at Gorgie in July 1926, having brought in the relief to the down 'Flying Scotsman', sometimes known as the 'Junior Scotsman'. Classified V1 by the North Eastern, this was one of a batch developed from Wilson Worsdell's Class V of 1903. C6 in the LNER list, the last was broken up in 1948. The two-cylindered V1s were not so highly rated as Sir Vincent Raven's Class 'Z' three cylindered Atlantics.

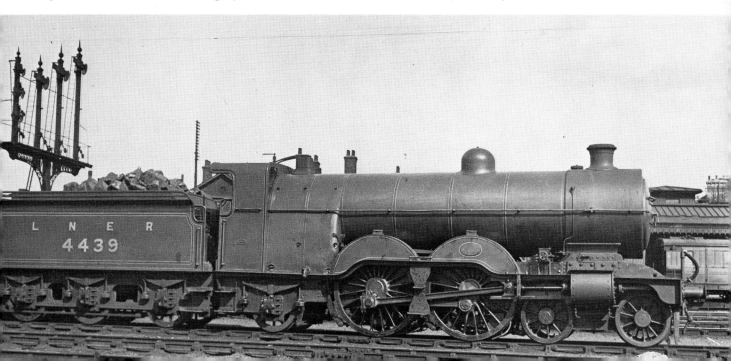

Newly arrived at Eastfield shed from Darlington in August 1928 is No. 329 *Inverness-shire*, one of six of the 'Shires' fitted with oscillating cam-operated Lentz poppet valves and classified D/49/3. Initially working from Perth shed, its performance was found to be unreliable and it was returned to Darlington for fitting with the standard Gresley 2-to-1 levers for the centre cylinder. After a further unsuccessful spell in Scotland, it was transferred to the flatter terrain of the North Eastern Area. In 1938, all six D49/3s were rebuilt with piston valves, bringing them into line with the original 'Shires' – D49 Part 1 – and in this form *Inverness-shire* returned to Scotland.

In complete contrast in the same location is Y9 0-4-0 saddle tank No. 9146 heading a pick-up goods from Portobello Yard. A regular working every Saturday afternoon, this was on occasions a remarkably heavy train for an engine weighing 28 tons, with only 14″ by 20″ cylinders. To a design by Neilson & Co., Glasgow, 44 of these engines were built for the NBR between 1882-99. In use all over the Southern Scottish Area, with a small wooden tender for coal attached according to the nature of their work, their 7′ wheelbase proved very useful in factory sidings or docks with restricted curves. Quite a few of these little engines saw service in British Railways days and one has been preserved in a museum in Lancashire.

Filling in for a Gresley Pacific, Raven 'Z' Atlantic No. 2205 (LNER C7) passes Craigentinny in 1929 on a down Leeds-Glasgow express. Later known as 'The North Briton', this train is composed of the final design of North Eastern express stock, bow-ended but not fitted with Pullman vestibules and buck-eye couplings. The second of the oddities at the front of the train is interesting. Built in York in 1905 for the East Coast Joint Service, the straight sides composed of narrow vertical strips without panelling below window level were described at the time as an attempt on the part of the GN and NE railways to save on construction costs. The complicated clerestory roof had also been replaced by a simple elliptical style. A lot of these were built before the appearance of the final ECJS high-roofed, bow-ended stock which became standard for the LNER for many years.

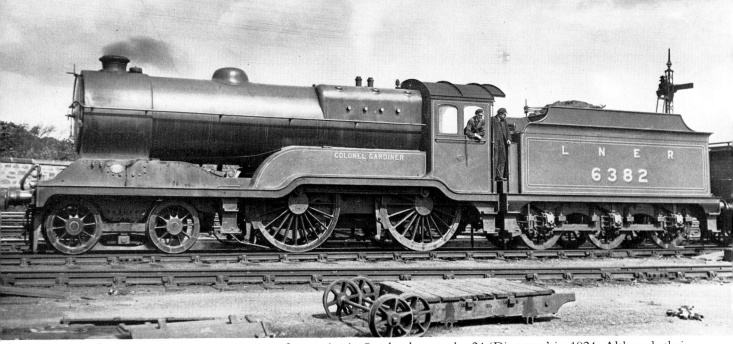

The first new post-Grouping engines for service in Scotland were the 24 'Directors' in 1924. Although their tractive effort was very similar to the Scotts, indeed sharing the same load classification – J – under the former NB scheme, their much larger boilers were greatly in their favour. Shedded at Haymarket, St. Margarets, Eastfield and Dundee, plus two at Perth, they immediately took over much of the main line work of the NB 4-4-0s. They were however, seldom found venturing to Carlisle, their 6'9" driving wheels being on the large side for the Waverley Route. No. 6382 *Colonel Gardiner,* photographed at Craigentinny in 1926 before black became their livery, shows the 'Scottish Director' at its best – apple green with the beautifully transferred name and the cut-away running plate.

N7 0-6-2T No. 2646, newly built by Beardmore & Co. in 1927 for working out of Liverpool Street, standing at Eastfield where all newly produced engines in the Glasgow area were initially delivered. These engines, a development of a well-known Great Eastern Railway design, had a new style of coal bunker as well as the extremely ugly 'Flower Pot' chimney which was applied to a lot of Robinson's engines on the Great Central in the early days of the Grouping.

N2 0-6-2T No. 897 and D51 4-4-0T No. 10429, photographed at Eastfield on a Saturday summer afternoon, represent the extremes in passenger tank engines in 1928 on former NB lines. Heavier rolling stock being provided for the suburban services in Edinburgh and Glasgow, something more powerful than the existing 4-4-2Ts was required which resulted in a number of Gresley's well-known 0-6-2Ts being built in 1925 and subsequently — classified, incidentally, in the Southern Scottish Area maximum load list as 'Metropolitan Type' — No. 897 has a chimney 4″ higher than those operating out of Kings Cross as well as the Westinghouse brake. No. 10429 is one of the little Drummond tanks already described in this volume, many of which were still in active service, not least on the Leith Central, Leith North and Gifford trains operating out of Waverley.

K3 2-6-0 No. 191 and J88 0-6-0T No. 9066 waiting in the weekend queue for entry to St. Margaret's shed on a Saturday afternoon at Craigentinny in 1926. The K3 was one of Gresley's famous three-cylinder 1000 class of 1918, 50 of which were built at Darlington in 1924–25, causing quite a stir when they appeared with typical NE style cabs in place of the former Ivatt design. Perhaps their most striking feature was the diameter of the boiler — six feet and far in excess of anything previously attempted at the time of building. The little tank with its dumb buffers, introduced in 1904, was W. P. Reid's first design for the NB. Sharing the same boiler with the D51 4-4-0T, some of them lasted nearly 56 years, unaltered in appearance except for the British Railways livery.

4-4-2T No.9448 was the ultimate in North British passenger tanks and is seen here in the black and red-lined livery adopted by the LNER for goods classes and tanks. Superheated developments of the No.1 class of 1911-13 twenty-one were constructed at Cowlairs 1915-21. All in all, this was a stylish-looking engine; retention of the smokebox wingplates helped to offset the prominent Westinghouse pump and might well have added some rigidity to the smokebox itself.

58

No.9896 *Dandie Dinmont*, a Scott dating from 1909, fresh from Cowlairs paintshop in 1928 and specially posed at Eastfield by helpful shed staff. This scene is perhaps suggestive of an engine restored ready for preservation in a museum, but in fact *Dandie Dinmont*, to be rebuilt with a superheated boiler in 1932, had another twenty years of service ahead. This photograph is an example of the early days when panchromatic material became available, in this case Ilford plate.

No. 2759 *Cumberland,* standing on No. 2 turntable at Eastfield, was one of eight D49/1 'Shires' built for Scotland in 1929, additional to the fifteen already there. Replacing the 'Directors' on intermediate express work, especially on the heavy Edinburgh and Glasgow expresses, they were useful substitutes for the Reid Atlantics, although their maximum permitted load was one coach less. All the Scottish counties covered by the LNER were represented in their names except Fife, although a *Fifeshire* had appeared in a list published by the company. Admittedly the hitherto desired '-shire' ending was unsuitable but at a time when engine naming was so much in vogue, *Kingdom of Fife* would have been splendid publicity. One 'Shire', No. 246 *Morayshire,* has been preserved and is now in the care of the Scottish Railway Preservation Society.

No. 14170, Whitelegg's rebuild of a Manson 4-4-0 design built 1892-1904, outside Hurlford shed in 1927. The cab, chimney and rather elaborate works plate were all new features for the Glasgow & South Western. Note the Caledonian semaphore signal on the buffer beam.

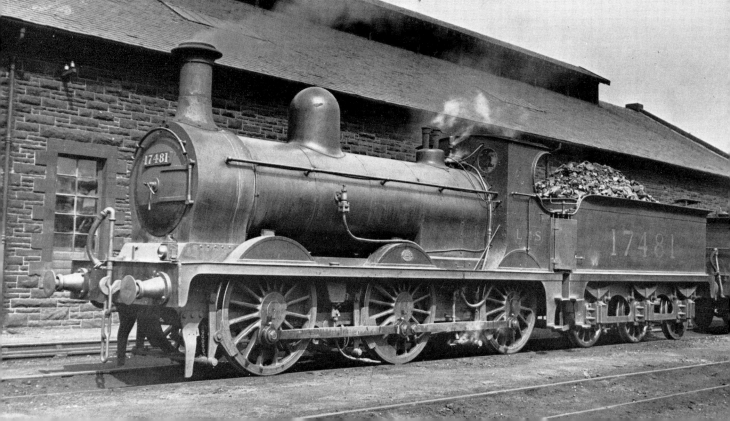

Three of Manson's 160 Class 0-6-0s built at Kilmarnock 1897-99 were rebuilt in 1926 with new boilers and Whitelegg design of cab. No.17201 was one of these, photographed also at Hurlford in 1927. It will be seen that the distinctive circular smokebox handrail introduced on the Baltics also appeared on these small engines.   Below, also seen at Hurlford is a larger Manson 0-6-0, No.17481, one of 34 engines built in the first decade of this century and still in original state. Known as the 361 class, they were the premier goods engines on the G&SW for many years. In 1920-25, twenty of the 361s were rebuilt with the X4 type boiler and Whitelegg cab.

No. 17514, one of Manson's final design of 0-6-0s, of which fifteen were built by the North British Locomotive Co. in 1910. A most efficient class, these remained the Glasgow & South Western premier goods engines for only three years, being overwhelmed by Peter Drummond's vast 0-6-0s of 1913.

HIGHLAND HOLIDAYS

A northbound local train at Kittybrewster station outside Aberdeen in July 1926, hauled by 4-4-0 No.6850 *Hatton Castle,* in perfect condition and shortly to be allocated for the annual visit of the Royal Train to Ballater. A sign of Inverurie's aim for perfection is the small plate covering the green-painted framing at the base of the smokebox, which tended to scorch on the superheated engines. The coaches making up the train, all GNoS origin, are a mixture of varnished teak and the pre-Grouping deep crimson and white. Behind the engine is one of the final design of Great North vestibuled corridors.

Specially selected to show the older type open cab is this photograph of Pickersgill 4-4-0 No. 6901, one of a class built in 1897 as a repetition of Johnson's design of four years earlier. These engines were noted for their fast running and on the 40 miles from Aberdeen to Huntly — by no means an easy road — speeds of up to 70 mph with 184 tons were recorded in 1896. Twenty-two saw service with British Railways, the last three being broken up in 1953.

No. 114, at Kittybrewster, was the second of Pickersgill's 4-4-0s which in 1899 introduced side-window cabs to the GNSR. Photographed early in 1924, the engine is still in the pre-Grouping livery of black with red and yellow lining. Ten of these engines had been ordered from Neilson Reid & Co., but after delivery of the first five, the Great North, involved in financial difficulties, found they could not accept the remaining engines. As a result, the builders sold them to the South Eastern & Chatham Railway, where they gave good service right into Southern Railway days.

No. 6848 *Andrew Bain,* a Heywood Class F 4-4-0 at Ballater, terminus of the Deeside line, in the final LNER style with the number on the cab-side in the beautifully shaded transfers which remained unaltered from 1923 until 1946 when the simpler Gill Sans style was adopted. The last engines built for the GNSR, all eight were named, six after Railway Officers or their residences. Andrew Bain was the Chairman, whilst *Hatton Castle,* on the previous page was the residence of G. A. Duff, the Deputy Chairman. Most aptly named was *Gordon Highlander,* honouring the Regiment so closely associated with Aberdeen and Great North Territory — and now preserved in Glasgow Transport Museum. Providing a pleasant background to this scene is the picturesque 1250' Craigendarroch — 'The Hill of the Oaks'.

In Highland and early LMS days, few expresses stopped between Perth and Blair Atholl. Passengers for such stations as Pitlochry had to make use of the Perth–Blair 'slows', such as this one at Pitlochry in 1927, bound for Perth. At the head is 'Loch' Class No. 14384 *Loch Laggan*, one of quite a large number of engines rebuilt or repaired in England in the final years of the Highland Railway. In this case Hawthorn, Leslie have fitted a boiler generally similar to the original, the main external difference being the flat dome and a chimney shortened by some essential repairs. This photograph conveys a true atmosphere of 'Derby Red', which is accentuated by coaches of Midland origin.

In or about 1929 several Horwich-built 2-6-0 'Crabs' were drafted to Perth North shed to augment the 'Rivers', 'Clans' and 'Castles' there. One of these Lancashire Moguls is shown heading a south-bound express through Kingussie with a rebuilt 'small Ben', No.14403 *Ben Attow*, acting as pilot. Attached at Aviemore, this will run through to the summit at Dalnaspidal, returning light engine to its home shed very likely with another pilot.

70

A southbound express at Grantown-on-Spey on the Forres line, the original route between Perth and Inverness prior to the construction of the direct link from Aviemore via Carr Bridge, which was finally opened on 1 November 1898. Five miles of the extremely scenic line between Aviemore and the Boat-of-Garten — all that remain of the 'Forres line' — are the venue of the Strathspey Railway today. No. 14684 *Duncraig Castle,* one of Peter Drummond's famous 'Castle' Class of 1900–10, was one of approximately fifteen engines equipped with Westinghouse brake by the Highland Railway for use on stock from its three neighbours, particularly the Great North, which was essentially a Westinghouse line. Note the large angles on the bufferbeam, fittings provided for the small snow ploughs universal on Highland engines during the winter months.

Some indications of the Engineer's weight limitations on the Highland Railway is reflected in the weight of the Cumming's 4-6-0 goods engine which exceeded the 56 tons of the earlier 'Jones Goods' by less than half a ton. Inevitably, the main dimensions were very similar but the Cumming engine had all the benefits of a design 24 years younger, with superheater and Walschaerts valve gear. Eight of these engines were built by Hawthorn, Leslie in 1918-19. Extremely useful, they were in operation on main line passenger work before more 'Clans' became available. It was probably on the Skye line, however, that they excelled and here they held premier place before being replaced by the Stanier Class 5. No.17951, illustrated here on duty at Inverness in 1929, was withdrawn in 1951.

73

A combination of the two Cumming passenger classes at Inverness in 1930: 4-4-0 No.14523 *Durn,* built in 1917, and 4-6-0 No.14766 *Clan Chattan,* one of the second batch of 'Clans' built in 1921. Both engines had arrived earlier with trains from Aberdeen and Perth respectively and, very fortunately, had been routed to the shed together when this photograph was taken.

No.17925, the last member of the famous 'Jones Goods' class built in 1894, and Britain's first 4-6-0, which was withdrawn in 1940 after a long life of 46 years; the engine is seen in its final form with Drummond chimney and after removal of smokebox wingplates. The glimpse of No.14393 *Loch Laoghal* shows the front end of both types at date of building, No.103, the first 'Jones Goods', now at Glasgow Transport Museum, having been modified accordingly. The two posts in the background of this scene at Aviemore in 1930 are reminders of the Highland Railway practice of raising their signal wires to keep them clear of drifting snow.

Shunting at Dingwall in August 1926 was No. 57B *Lochgorm,* built in 1872 by David Jones to the design of Stroudley's 0-6-0T of 1869. The water tank arched over the boiler and solid centres to the middle driving wheels added to the quaint appearance of this little engine, which has a Jones type chimney without louvres. Its final days, when it was numbered 16119, were spent in shunting at Inverness shed, withdrawal taking place in 1934.

'Skye Bogie' 4-4-0 No. 14282, coaling at Dingwall shed in August 1927, was one of four built 1897-1901 which brought the total of the class to nine engines. Completed after David Jones' retirement by his successor Drummond, various modifications included the latter's style of chimney instead of the louvred type carried by the earlier engines. This photograph was taken at a time when the 'Skye Bogie' was the mainstay of the Kyle line, No. 14282 with two others being shedded at Kyle of Lochalsh and a fourth at Dingwall. In addition, at Dingwall was a small 'Ben' — No. 14412 *Ben Avon* — used exclusively on the 'Mail', the forenoon train from Inverness and its return working. All in well-kept LMS red, they were a delight to the eye.

A rare and unusual visitor to Dingwall in the early 1930s was LNWR Webb 'coal tank' No.7727, tried on the Strathpeffer branch. This was not the first English pre-Grouping type to be stationed there, as in the 1914–18 War Adams 4-4-2Ts from the LSWR worked to Kyle. Moreover, half a century later an ex-GWR Pannier tank from the closed Dornoch branch spent some time shunting at Dingwall and was then the last steam engine in active service on the former Highland Railway.   [W. D. M. Stephen]

A local from Tain to Inverness leaving Dingwall Junction in August 1926, behind 'Big Ben' No. 14417 *Ben Na Caillach*. Built in 1908 by the North British Locomotive Co, this was the last of the class to remain in original condition, being rebuilt with superheater and Urie extended smokebox a year after this photograph was taken.

A southbound express at Aviemore in August 1929, headed by 4-6-0s No.14769 *Clan Cameron* and No.14682 *Beaufort Castle*. The small Westinghouse pump on the 'Castle' goes back to Highland days; the 'Clan' with a very much larger one, had been Westinghouse fitted when through running to Buchanan Street took place for a period in the early days of the Grouping. Below; *Clan Cameron* again, photographed at Kingussie in 1927 on a Perth-Inverness express.

Deputising for the usual branch engine at Strathpeffer, in August 1926, was No.16118, Stroudley's 0-6-0T built in 1869 — a design which has come to be regarded as the prototype of the LBSCR 'Terriers'. This was the only engine built for the Highland during Stroudley's stay there, the two others of the class being added subsequently by David Jones. No.16118 differed from *Lochgorm* in having solid wheels on all three axles plus larger tanks fitted in 1902 for the Dornoch branch. The train is a delightful mixture of Highland, Midland and LNWR stock, the latter carriage, in umber and white, being the through coach from Inverness. The leading coach, with 'Perth & Aberfeldy' painted on the solebars, was a superior six-wheeler design for the through service from Perth and was attached to the Aberfeldy branch train at Ballinluig Junction. Note that the roof ventilators were provided for smoking compartments only. The elegant and well-roofed station was complementary to the palatial railway-owned Highland Hotel.

Two designs were built by the NBR for use on the West Highland Railway, the first being Matthew Holmes' 'West Highland Bogies', a 5ft. 7in. driving wheel version of his main line express engine. Twelve were built in 1894 for the opening of the line to Fort William in August of the same year. Finally totalling 24 engines, and not very successful, they were not rebuilt — with the exception of No.695 — as were most of the Holmes main line 4-4-0s. Thus only seven engines entered LNER service, where they ended their days chiefly in banking duties. No.341, photographed at Dunbar in 1920, assisted trains on the Cockburnspath bank: the efficient tender cab was most desirable on the long tender-first return trip from the summit. This was one of my earliest photographs and I recall the difficulty I had in persuading the engine crew and shed staff not to stand in a too obviously posed position along the entire length of the engine. . . .

The second design synonymous with the West Highland and also in service throughout the NBR was the famous 4-4-0 'Glen' class, thirty-two of which were built 1913-20. Standing at Eastfield in 1928, No. 9100 *Glen Dochart* illustrates the class at its best in LNER green and at a time when they were building up an excellent reputation for handling the increasingly heavy passenger traffic on the West Highland. Standard NB main line corridors were replacing the shorter and lighter stock specially built for the line and another innovation was the Sunday excursion which brought restaurant cars to Fort William for the first time. These the 'Glens' handled in pairs, the maximum double headed load for the line being 300 tons. Displaced by Gresley 2-6-0 types, the 'Glens' continued in active service on other lines, including former GNSR territory, until 1961 when all but No. 256 *Glen Douglas* were withdrawn. This locomotive now remains as a memory in Glasgow Transport Museum.

SCOTTISH MEDLEY

For the neighbouring Callander and Oban line, the Caledonian provided three special classes, Brittain's 'Oban Bogies' of 1882, McIntosh's 4-6-0s of 1902 and finally Pickersgill's 4-6-0s of 1922. No.14103, station shunter at Stirling in 1927, was quite a museum piece as, although rebuilt by McIntosh, the only striking difference was his chimney replacing a plain stove-pipe style. The four-wheel tender on the last three of the class which survived until 1930 was also unique at the time. The numerous posts in the background caused problems for a photographer but fortunately it was possible to keep the outlines of the chimney and dome unimpaired. The Pickersgill 4-6-0s, his last engines built for the Caledonian Railway, are represented at Oban shed in 1923 by No.195 (above), then quite new and looking extremely smart in Caledonian blue. As is well-known, these engines did not live up to expectations and in the 1930s were replaced by Highland 'Clans'. These in their turn were later superseded by the Stanier Class Five.

84

Caledonian 2-6-0 No.36 was one of five engines with 19½in. × 26in. cylinders and 5ft. coupled wheels built in 1912 by McIntosh for the CR. Based on an earlier, heavy 0-6-0, a leading pair of wheels was added to ease the weight at the front end, resulting in an unusual and somewhat ungainly looking engine. Mostly employed south of Glasgow, No.36 was an unusual visitor to Perth where it was photographed in July 1924 still in CR goods livery, black with red and white lining. None of the class was rebuilt, the last to be withdrawn being No.38 – 17804 – which was broken up in 1937.

Another oddity, again on the G&SWR, was the eight-wheeled tender carried partly on bogie and partly on fixed wheels, two of which were built by Manson for use on a service with limited stops. One of these is shown fitted to No. 14248, one of his 240 class of 1904, photographed at Hurlford in 1927. The same designer had previously built six similar tenders for the GNSR, one of which at least survived until 1925.

A second Scottish 2-6-0 appeared in 1915, designed by Peter Drummond for the G&SWR and again a development of a large 0-6-0 design. These two inside-cylindered 2-6-0 classes, so similar below running plate level, were unique in British locomotive practice. No.17827 was photographed at the former CR shed at Stirling in 1926, usually left on an unattended turntable due to difficulties in turning – the driver and fireman having gone for assistance. This scene records the first LMS goods livery – black with LMS red based panel on cabside and large numerals on tender.

This photograph, taken at Inverkeithing in 1920, illustrates the first locomotive constructed for the recently formed Royal Air Force. The builders, Andrew Barclay Sons & Co., of Kilmarnock, despatched this powerful 12in. × 20in. 0-6-0T — the only one built — to R.A.F. Donibristle in April 1920. No. 1 worked on a railway between the aerodrome and a jetty at Inverkeithing used for conveying stores and equipment to naval ships lying in the Forth. In the right background are the cantilevers of the Forth Bridge.

Concluding this trio of tank engines is Gresley N2 0-6-2T No.4729 going all-out past Inverkeithing East Junction on an Edinburgh-Kirkcaldy Sunday local. Condensing gear had been removed on its transfer from suburban work in the London area and Westinghouse brakes had been fitted. Note that GN style indicator boards on the smokebox are in use.

Another Barclay-built industrial locomotive, photographed in 1928 in a new coat of green paint, was owned by Caldwells, papermakers of Inverkeithing. The very crude looking cab, which left little room for the driver, was an improvement on the weatherboard style to be seen on similar engines lying derelict in colliery sidings in the 1920s. On the embankment in the background of this photograph can be seen the LNER main line to the North.

Eyes on the signal and waiting to give the 'right away', the guard stands at the head of the down 'Royal Scot' at Carlisle (Kingmoor) after a change of engines following the 299.1 mile non-stop run from Euston. Taking the train on to Glasgow is 'Royal Scot' No.6129 *Comet* complete with Caledonian semaphore on the smokebox front.

On the East Coast, 'The Flying Scotsman' nears the end of its non-stop run of 392.7 miles from Kings Cross to Waverley and is photographed here in 1929 passing Portobello West signal box. The engine is Haymarket A3 Pacific No.2566 *Ladas*. This summer service held the record for the longest regular run without a stop, made possible of course by the Gresley corridor tender. On special test runs the LMS also completed the 401.4 miles from Euston to Glasgow Central without any stop.

Gresley's high-pressure four-cylinder 4-6-4 No. 10000, fitted with Yarrow water tube boiler (w.p. 450lb per sq. in.) photographed at Haymarket in February 1930. At this date tests were conducted from that shed, the most important being a return trip to Perth on Sunday, 23 February 1930. The train consisted of 13 coaches including the LNER dynamometer car, weighing in all 406 tons – a vast load for the Glenfarg bank with its ruling gradient of 1 in 74 for more than six miles. This run received little publicity in the railway press but newspaper reports, which gave great prominence to the engine's nickname 'Hush Hush' – due to the secrecy attending its construction – are interesting. On the train were William Whitelaw (LNER Chairman), H. N. Gresley and his principal assistant for many years, O. V. S. Bulleid. On the outward journey the train was 26 minutes late on schedule at Perth although allowances must be made for a photographic stop on the Forth Bridge, also a stop on the severe rising gradient at Dunfermline Lower. Little information about the tests was ever made available other than they were highly satisfactory. Later in 1930, No. 10000 was reported working on an ordinary Gateshead link including one return trip on the non-stop 'Flying Scotsman'. In 1937 Gresley converted her into a three-cylinder simple on the lines of his A4 but still retaining the unusual wheel arrangement.

A rear view of the Gresley corridor tender showing the buck-eye coupling in swung down position when not in use, also the spare screw type coupling for other stock. The port-hole provided light for the corridor (5ft. high and 18in. wide) through which the crews passed to change over *en route*. The engine is A3 Pacific No. 4476 *Royal Lancer*, one of the three Kings Cross Pacifics fitted with these tenders for the commencement of the non-stop runs in May 1928, when this photograph was taken at Haymarket.

Photographs of three premier passenger types on shed at Carlisle in 1929. These magnificent engines all appeared within a period of six years and are interesting to compare. Foremost is Gresley A3 Pacific No.2749 *Flamingo* which with two others had recently arrived at Canal shed to take over Waverley Route expresses, which for so long had been in the most capable hands of the Reid Atlantics. *Flamingo* was allocated to Canal a few weeks after completion in 1929 and was to remain there until withdrawal in 1961, by that date numbered 60095. These three Gresleys were the pride of Canal, as is evident from the splendid condition of *Flamingo* posed by Driver Wildey. The 'Royal Scot' 4-6-0s, built by the North British Locomotive Co. in Glasgow in 1927, caused a considerable sensation with their huge boilers, minute chimneys and generally bold outline — marred unfortunately by the relatively small, narrow Midland tender. No.6139 *Ajax* has just arrived at Kingmoor having brought the 'Royal Scot' on its non-stop run from Euston. What appear to be baulks of wood on the tender suggest that there has been a little building up to increase the coal space in the tender. As is well known, the class received large capacity Stanier tenders in later years. Concluding the trio, No.14803 is one of Pickersgill's three-cylinder 4-6-0s which by 1929 had been relegated to goods traffic. A fundamental difference in this express passenger design was the diameter of the driving wheels, which, compared with the 6ft. 8in. of the Pacific and 6ft. 9in. of the Royal Scot, was only 6ft. 1in. — at that time regarded as more suitable for mixed traffic work. Splendid looking machines with great potentialities, they must have been on the drawing board simultaneously with the Gresley Pacific but with sadly different results. But for the Grouping surely their faults could have been remedied, as has happened to so many other designs in the past.

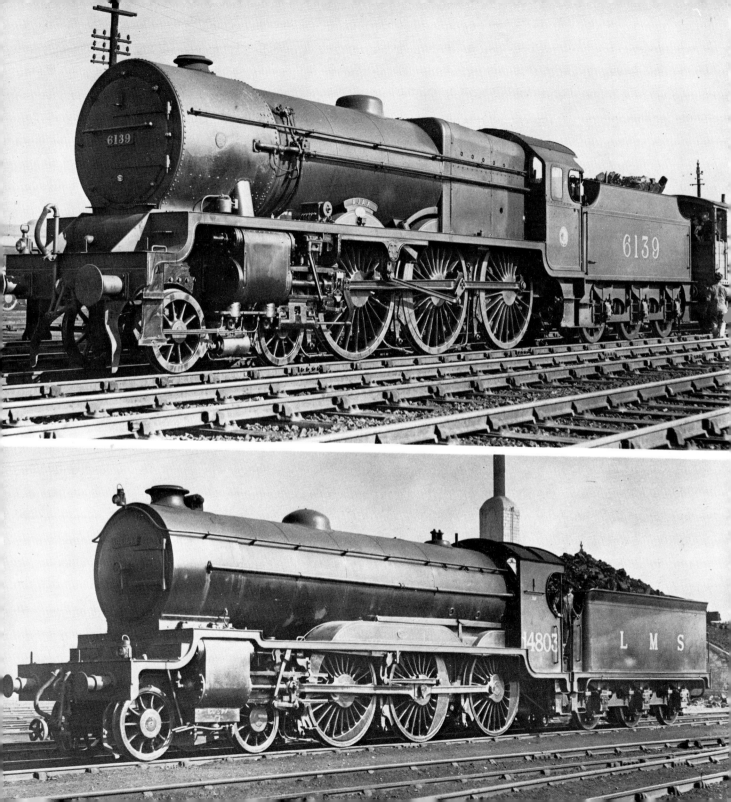

Two hundred miles or so further north from the large trio at Carlisle, a little 'Skye Bogie' — weighing with tender a mere 73 tons — approaches Fodderty Junction, the former junction for the now closed Strathpeffer Branch with a goods train for Kyle of Lochalsh. At this point the railway runs parallel to the A832, the main road to Ullapool and the Western Isles. 4-4-0 No.14284, sharing the same red livery as the 'Royal Scot' on the previous page, is another of the four turned out by Drummond after David Jones had left the Highland. It was the last to be broken up — in 1930.

© copyright D. Bradford Barton 1977 □ ISBN 0 85 153 279 9 □ Set in Monotype Bembo and printed by offset litho by H. E. Warne Ltd, of London and St. Austell, for the publishers D. Bradford Barton Ltd, of Trethellan House, Truro, Cornwall.